Pique | Ennui

C.L Phillips

ISBN: 979-8-8389-6790-9

Dedication

To the little girl who wanted to write fairytales but ended up writing this.

Contents

As my body recovers and I survive
An ode to the writer
Apathetic in a new way
Honestly, I'm frightened
Finally
Sorry isn't the right word, but.

Preface

I remember a conversation when I was a wannabee-writer as a kid. I'd overheard the saying 'write what you know' and I was stumped. What did I have to tell the world? What could I ink that was exciting, horrifying, or inspiring? Perhaps I manifested wanting experiences beyond my youth a little too keenly.

This anthology came into being not because of the things that I've witnessed or that have happened to me but because of what I decided to do with those experiences. I found myself edging away from romanticism and following the path into the dark, gritty truths. I began writing for me because as many writers and indeed non-writers do, I felt oppressed- like the world didn't want to hear what I had to say. Then gradually, the opposite came true. I looked at my favorite authors; they were people who inspired me, comforted me, or made me feel seen. Although the anthology may be unsettling or uncomfortable at times, I wanted to create a space in which the stigmas or shame of trauma didn't have a place in the narrative.

The anthology is formatted as an emergence from my own chrysalis- it isn't linear and at times it's suffocating but by the end of the book, I'm coming out the other side.

The pivotal thing to keep in mind when reading this anthology, is that there are moments or poems in which I don't recognize myself. As an entirety, the anthology represents my journey but individually, each poem speaks to a feeling or opinion at that moment in time.

Pique, the first half of the anthology begins with *Priorities* and ends at *Then.* Its themes are quite morbid, somewhat vulgar and at times disturbing. This is done purposefully as a transition into the latter half of the anthology, *Ennui.* Although a shorter collection of poems, it is here that the narrative moves into the present.

Take from this anthology what you want, read as much or as little as you can stomach. If you're not at the place to read it yet, don't worry- I wasn't when I was writing it. But I hope someday you will be.

-Chloe.

Priorities

I remember being younger,
ten or thirteen.
Laying in my bed,
thinking about how God had created me
(because that's what I believed at the time)
and wondering;
what if he hadn't?
A sinking, panicked feeling.
Cold right to my toes,
like I'd just been submerged
into ice
that melted,
drowning: I'd never rise to the surface.
The thought of me not existing,
terrifying.
But then what?
I supposed it would be dark,
wherever it was you lingered
if you weren't here.
I was too naïve to comprehend
I was contemplating life and death.

I tried, years later
to reach that bleak, all-consuming worry
but I couldn't,
no matter how far I retreated into my mind,
bring myself to fret.
I know now, of course
that the sadness I'd felt
at the thought of being without my family-
at never eating chocolate again-
or not knowing what it felt like to dream while sleeping-
didn't feel half as scary as it did then.

I guess I realised
bodies are temporary.
They rot without your permission.
Most times the flesh goes first.
The heart stops pumping,
or the lungs run out of air.
But sometimes,

as it was for me,
the mind goes first.
Apathetic, you leave your body
for that gloomy void
you were once so afraid of
and it's more ruinous than you could ever have
imagined.

Yours for tonight

We met in the dark.
Strangers fumbling, trying to fix
the broken parts of ourselves
by slamming our bodies together
like an aggressive toddler with a jigsaw.

I would cry out "I'm all yours,"
clutching your head to my heart-
or my tits,
as we rocked together
like a toy sailboat in a bathtub.

But I was only giving myself away
in the casual sense.
Fleetingly, letting you hold me
only as tightly
as the string of a kite in a storm.

Then day would dutifully come
and I'd become my own again.
Alone, like I wanted, I'd realise
in hiding from the glare of being seen,
I missed seeing you.

Versatile

"Kiss me" lipstick and "fuck me" liner
or "baby faced" blush and "baby doll" lashes.
the daily decision between
being sexualised or infantilised.

Woman: like a chameleon,
adjusting to phallocentric situations.
Doesn't matter how prey presents
because both versions have a hole to fuck.

Shrinking into skin-tight clothes,
more appealing to the predator.
The perfidious power of feeling wanted,
replacing the vehement fear of being hunted.

Mouse

Cheap drinks, spilling secrets like disclaimers.
Bathroom sinks, splashing water like party streamers.

Reality hits when your heads in your hands
 and arse on the toilet.
I shouldn't have said that, I shouldn't be here
but keeping quiet
because you don't want to spoil it.

The quiet that comes when everyone's laughing or crying,
existing amongst friends, the best distraction from feeling like dying.

Cursing through cramps as you reach for the loo roll,
finding there's none left.
Dry mouth, sticky skin, blurred vision
as you return to memories being made,
living feels like theft.

You pour another drink, shaking from a few seconds sobered up.
Sick in your mouth- don't throw up- chugging vodka from your cup.

The conversation's changed and you can't find your place.
Tongue grown too big
for words too long and too many,
and too wrong
as you bum from a cig.

You wonder what it's like to have thoughts, not just feelings.
To give your opinion on topics, instead of staring at ceilings.

It's weird,
 the things that make you feel alive
are from observation.
Not participation.

Ante-mortem

That summer, flies clung to me in the heat,
like they knew my dreadful secret.
Testing my skin's nest,
as though perusing an abandoned property.

The sunshine separated itself
in an invisible veil,
afraid to scorch my fragile flesh
or lay light on a hideous truth.

The rain was kind to me when it came,
lashing down without mercy.
Cold droplets on a corpse,
leaking life like ink into my veins.

The flies resided on our windows those months,
spectators to a funeral procession.
First-come-first served.
Even then my body was not my own.

Manwhore, the mutilated muse

Manwhore.
The mutilated muse.
I linger in my loathing, liking, loving-
it's all mixed up.
Because without it, the pages are blank.
And I'm just a bitter bitch,
sitting at her keyboard.
Swiping without interest on Tinder,
checking if you've replied.
Changing my Instagram bio,
checking if you've replied.
Ignoring all other messages,
checking if you've replied.
But definitely not writing.

Cost of sinning

An inadequate justice really,
to castrate the corrupt
when it is their foul mind
that has caused the most hurt.
As if ridding them of their 'manhood'
takes away their power
or the source of her fear.
To remove a hood from a car,
may stop it functioning in the physical sense,
but is no less a motor-
a vehicle of weight, force, and grease,
And so to remove the hood from a man,
may stop it forcing its way in
to the core that it craves,
but man's depravity can still indulge in her mind.
Better a lobotomy instead.

Author note: This poem was written from a place of bitterness towards a specific persons. It in no way is meant to be a generalisation of those identifying as men or to express any such views.

Sedate and placate

Curb-side conversations.
Wrong place, wrong time, wrong man.
Lighter flickering between your fingers,
sooner burn me than hold my hand.
Your words are like radio static,
noisy and out of place.
But I steal glances of my lipstick on your lips,
my trace on your face.

Something about you doesn't sit right in my head
but we move from the pavement
and you pound me in your bed,
let me escape that drowning sense of dread.

When we fuck, I sigh "oh god."
Not because I want him to answer
but because I'd rather moan his name
than yours.
Your name feels like a password
to a part of you I don't deserve.
So I gasp, whimper, howl
a white noise reverb.

It's pathetic you think you know me
from your hands between my legs.
Prying me apart, like a watermelon
with a blunt knife.

I feel your tongue,
tiptoeing across my torrid flesh.
Licking my wounds only to deepen the sore,
fingers jamming up against my rotten core.
And I, afraid of appearing hostile, writhe away
but beg for more.
A string of innocence, hooked in your index, being slowly unravelled,
tangled, knotted, then left the mess it was before.

Feelings dispenser

Tuesday, you met a tiny fragment of me.
Copper curly hair, awkward and shifty.
In the midst of deconstructing,
I had nothing of me to offer you
except rehearsed replies and a dry smile.
I gave enough away that you'd call me
lovely
but wouldn't want to see me again.
The type of timid that was boring,
occasioned by half-interesting blurtings
and somewhat alive laughs.
Hints that I had been or could be
vivacious, charming, witty
without tempting you to find out.

Yet somehow I ended up seeing you again
and this time the fracture
sealed itself a little.
An exterior, aesthetic finish,
eclipsing the inward barrenness
in its floating, flirty veil.
Paranoid and panicked
that the wind would blow
and throw open the shutters,
I retreated from the window.
Leaving behind a cloud of dust
that caught in the back of your throat,
like cigarette smoke and ashes in the breeze.
Lingering, but barely present.

Each time we spoke I offered you more
of my cracked, sporadic self,
hoping you would piece it back together
and I'd become whole in your hands.
This excitement was erratic,
founded in the archaic belief
that a man could fix a woman.
But cavemen weren't known for love.
Things didn't become bigger
under scrutiny
but rather the small imperfections were magnified.

I was both patient and doctor,
addict and dealer
- wondering which would survive.

Until the hammer dropped
on the agitated, ticking clock's face.
And instead of time slowing
or speeding up,
the hourglass filling
or draining.
The tiny fragment shattered.
Shards were swept away
and the elapsed was meaningless.

Close-knit

You have nicknames for your friends.
You don't waste your breath for syllables, on those you cherish.
But you moan my name, you wear it out.
It's a filler between breaths and groans, transferrable and thoughtless,
tumbling from your lips as easy as a sink overflowing.
Because your seconds with me don't matter so much.
They're just moments, not memories
and your words only add up to the purpose
of getting me into your bed.

I think I want to be your friend, more than I want to sleep with you.
I hate my name. You've made mine dirty
and theirs precious.
Theirs worthy
and mine worthless.
An empty gasp against your whiskey glass.

Say it.
Call me something soft.
In a calmer tone.
Say it.
Please.
Just once.

The devil wears pyjamas

It never occurred to me that you wear pyjamas.
In my mind, you were a perfect sculpture.
The James Dean I'd heard my mother fawn over.
A rich man dressing in poor man fashion;
individual items that cost more than my entire outfit.

I made you a God, and so you acted like one.
A daddy deity, looking down on me,
even though you were 2 inches shorter.
But every holy scripture is worthless when torn apart
and as I flipped through your pages and rhetoric,
your enticements seemed more like bribes.

You were perfect, when put-together and presented,
but picked apart you came back deficient.
I was embarrassed when you got things wrong,
presuming you were right. Or when you let slip
your serpent tongue.
Embarrassed not by your unwarranted cockiness, but
by my uneducated, unfaltering confidence in you.

The devil wears pyjamas, not snake-skin or prada.
And I see why Eve was tempted.

you, you, you

you.
The virus that validates me, makes me vain.
but the last person to see me vulnerable and reassure me.
I'm used to men wanting to fuck me,
but I'm scared when they want to be my friend.
What do you offer the narcissistic nihilist who has everything?
----
you.
Made me feel like I was enough.
but turns out I'm too much.
Because crazy is hot;
adrenaline, endorphins, dopamine. A temporary high.
You crossed my heart and hoped I'd die.
----
you.
Let me chase you like a bitch in heat,
knowing I was the type of girl
who'd get on her knees if you told her.
But would run rabid, wild, afraid,
instead of being a lapdog at your feet.

Unlovely

I think I'm getting uglier every day,
rotting from the inside out.
A carcass rebuilt turns puffy and blotchy,
pressure mounting in my bloated abdomen.

My secrets are excreted in the blood
of my gums when I floss too hard.
Choked back down by perfume, candles
and chewing gum.

Nails broken and brittle,
from scraping my feelings to the surface,
like dead fireflies floating
in a kiddies pool.

Nothing hotter than the scent of arson on my lips
and my summer body creeping up my throat.
It's stained teeth, scratchy voice season.
Hayfever, or something.

The big 'oh'

I loosened my heart and you loosened your trousers.
Your reassurances like threats,
darting out of your rusty bullet mouth,
without hesitation, intent with consequence.

Skin on skin, scratches on thighs.
Playing with fire,
instead of running with knives.

An orgasm a day keeps suicide away
or at least that was your solution.
When apathetic and pathetic I told you,
I didn't really feel like living
and you took me to your bed,
showed me what I'd be missing.

"You can talk to me", you said after
your hand had been wrapped around my throat.
But moans came easier than words
and the self-disgust and guilt that followed
was a welcome reprise from detestation
and disassociation.

Strangers I feel close to

I think I see you in the street,
every time I watch a peach-fuzzed man-child
hold a lighter to a new era twiggy's fag.
And brush her hair behind her ears,
sheltering it from the smoke and fire.
Stroking her cheek, as gently as a silk scarf floating in a breeze.
Then I remember, you would never touch me that way in public.

I think I hear you calling my name,
every time a misplaced accent rings throughout the pub.
Asking the football score, or debating independence
with a stranger who only knows
one side of the wall.
Saying your piece and disrupting my peace.
Then I remember, I'd have nothing worthwhile to reply.

Every time I feel that.
Elevated heartbeat,. Ecstatic, electric energy.
The temporary fixation I know won't last
and shouldn't have such a hold over me.
I take out my phone and look at that one picture.

I really hate that one picture of you.
The one that reminds me of the you
I knew before we met.
The perfect you I imagined,
but I'm starting to forget.

But little moments like this
give me déjà vu of you
and who I want you to be.
How I want you to be with me.
How I want the world to see
us kissing in that fucking street.

Sweet-tooth

Honey dripping- ink blot- black coffee pot.
Busy bees- time wasted- ungrateful mug.
Lipstick-stained rim- cherry pips in my teeth.
Juice trickling down my chin- pulp on my tongue.

I know I can be bitter
but I have a sweet tooth
for you
and that's a hard fact
to swallow.

The bad place

I am the bad place.

In the way that the dentist's chair is the bad place.
How the rubber gloves squeak against your teeth and the scraping probe pin pricks blood from your gums.
How a strangers breath seeps through their mask against your forehead and you swear you can feel the seat reclining until your hair is touching the bleach-covered floor.

In the way that club toilets are the bad place.
Your nose stuffed with the stench of sweaty bodies and spilt tequila.
Sobering up when you're staring down the toilet bowl like it's a mirror.

In the way that a fisherman's boat in a storm is the bad place.
High tides and high tensions, how people become heroic or hostile in a split second.
When you're abandoned to the skies or the sea, being rained down on or drowning down below.

I am the bad place.
I see people at their worst.
And they see me as an experience they'd rather forget.

Smaller, subtler, calmer

There's been times when I've wanted to be
smaller, subtler, calmer.
Like a leech to my lover's quicksand skin,
or dust on an old duvet.
To see and to feel,
without being seen or felt.
To breathe without thinking,
to stare without blinking,
to be high without drinking,
to be safe without shrinking.

But then there was the time I wanted to be,
bigger, louder, bolder.
When your fist collided with the wall
outside the o2 academy
and every hair on my body
screamed out braver than I ever could.

On the walk then to the bus stop,
my friends and I shaking,
silence began breaking and we laughed-
a laugh like shouting out I love you.
I heard their heartbeats then,
above any thoughts in my head.
I realised then that feelings can be
known, without ever being said.

Her and me

I feel like I'm lying to a part of me.
The paper-cut patch, plastered part of me
that knows better, knows I deserve better.
The part of me that knows for every time
you kiss my cheek and tell me I'm pretty,
you're thinking of her.

And then there's moments when finally, I'm honest.
When I lay my head on your pillow
and realise there's a hair that isn't mine,
brushing against my jaw.
Knowing then you've laid like this with her,
breathing the same air.

But it's easier to forget.
Tell myself it's in the past,
that in a couple of weeks,
when your skin is new, uncharted territory,
and you press your forehead to mine,
it'll be like I'm the only person you've ever touched.

The chase

I thought I liked it.
The flirting without consequence,
the kisses without meaning,
sex without rules.
I thought I liked the chase,
until I saw her cross the finish line before me,
You double-knotting her thin wrists in red ribbon,
while I fumble with my loose laces,
stuck at the starting point.

And it's not your fault.
I never tried to smudge the chalk from the ground.
I etched the line myself,
setting myself up for failure
because I never thought for a minute
I could win.

But here,
catching my breath between congratulations and commiserations.
I don't feel that I've been defeated,
as much as the race was rigged.

Routine

Coming home, how quickly you
fall back into a routine.

Yoga mat in the living room,
weights tucked under your bed.

Dishes done before 6,
dog walked after brunch.

Chastising your shitty town,
while you chase 10,000 steps.

Body-checking 24/7,
panicked breathing lulling you to sleep.

Silent wars on your side of the dinner table,
phone on airplane mode.

Googling cheap flights,
guilt-tripped out of booking them.

Chapped lips,
chipped nail polish.

Brushing your teeth every hour,
to taste nothing and feel skinny.

Dying your hair every week,
only for it to fall out every morning.

Watching amateur porn,
taking scolding showers to stop the shame.

Sexting someone for validation,
feeling more insecure after.

Having a double measure,
getting stressed and smoking.

Covering your mirror just far enough,
that you can still do your eyeliner.

Finishing books you hate,
just to be anywhere but here.

Then

Leaving home, how difficult
it is to make new habits.

Freedom feels restricting,
choosing nothing over making a decision,

Craved independence is overwhelming,
clinging to the wrong person.

Resting is a test,
burn out the aspiration.

Coming home again because
you can't get better on your own.

Commitment issues

I'm now afraid of the word forever.
Hearing it is like having a gun pulled to my head,
or poison dripping from glass to tongue,
threatening to take everything away.
It's funny how things can travel
from person to person.
One moment passed round, infecting like a virus.

I wonder where you found it-
that dirty, cracked hourglass
just waiting-
to shatter.
I wonder why you picked it up,
if you shivered when you held it in your hands,
if you knew what it was capable of.

I can't blame you, for trapping me in your timepiece.
I'd already left my footprints in the sand,
tasted the saltwater in my mouth.
But it still hurt,
you burying me, watching me drown-
feeling my scream without me making a sound.

And when you've grieved me
and left the bedside of my grave-
a martyr will come,
claw at the sand, breath air into my soaked lungs.
They'll grab me by my curled up hand,
promise to love me
and leave their own mark in the sand.
Wondering always what hides inside my clenched up fist
and finally prying it open
to find the pearl in the clam.
An hourglass-
a gift from me to them.

Then

I opened my eyes,
scarcely remembering willing them
to turn away from you.

and your brown boots on the floor
as I stretch across the mattress.
cold leather brushing against fingertips,

the sensation travelling from those to toe.
that first sip of water in the morning,
when your throat is dry and scratchy

has come to be ignored.
replaced by your mouth on mine,
clumsy but content.

your sleep-drunk eyes,
unarmoured and naked
as your glasses gather dust on the ground.

I almost fall asleep again
with your head on my chest
and my hands in your hair.

but slanted blinds slip in
morning light,
blazing and unaware
of what she's interrupted.

'Survivor'

And it's closed now-
that door I've been pushed up against for too long.
Finally, the weight I was feeling crashed through it
and left me outside.
I thought it'd feel freeing
but my skin's splintered and I'm tired.
I've went from suffocation to isolation,
either way I can't breathe.

The system

The form asks how I'm feeling.
"nothing" is too short an answer,
"everything" takes up too many lines.
So I nitpick through, choosing what's
necessary and negligent to mention.

I wish there was a scan, a sample or a swab.
Instead of a tickbox test, interrogation,
forcing to the surface every introspection.

The nurse asks me how I'm feeling.
I say "where do I start?"
It's all ups and downs, tears and laughs
with no linear chart.
She notes it all down, sighs, says it's a lot,
like I don't know.

It feels weird saying it aloud.
I grimace at how bad it sounds, tumbling from my lips out of rhyme.
Feeling guilty and insecure, like I'm wasting their time.

The doctor asks how I'm feeling.
I tell him just enough,
that I won't be rushed into the ward,
but they'll give me pills to pass me off.
Because that's how we treat a sickness.

So the secret's out. I'm exposed.
That's the hardest part, they said. But they're wrong.
Confiding was relieving, until half an hour ended, and I'm told to
move along.

As my body recovers and I survive

I let tiny, insignificant parts of me die.
My hair splitting from root to end, clogging up the drain,
and my nail beds cracked and splintered, picking at them again.
My teeth turned yellow like mustard
and my gums red like cranberry.
My skin cold and prickly, like a hedgehog in fright,
and my elbows grazed and jagged, arms bruised in the light.
I let these tiny, insignificant parts of me die-
so it feels like a victory every day my brains still alive.

An ode to the writer

Little me; curly haired and chubby cheeked
would be so disappointed in me.

She'd be disappointed that we never got that fish tattoo on our ring finger. That we never grew our hair out. That we gave up the idea that a stage could be home. That bff's really only meant best friends for a bit.

but you know what?
sometimes I am so angry at her.

I'm angry at her for not taking a breath
when things felt too big. For the never-ending tick of her brains internal clock.
For every time she kept her mouth shut when she knew the answer. For spitting out chicken in the toilet bowl. For being more mature then, than I ever will be now. And god I'm jealous- of all the things she didn't know and didn't want to know. I know too much now.

but mostly I feel sorry
for the both of us.

I'm sorry that when we weren't the tubby kid anymore, we still didn't feel small enough. I'm sorry that your perfectly brushed teeth are now yellow. I'm sorry that I've forgotten how to deter a tantrum by using 'big girl words'. I'm sorry that I still don't know what our favourite book or movie is. I'm sorry that I can't write fairytales, but I promise I will try to tell the truth.

And I hope,
I can make us proud.

I hope I can find the magic in the woods again. I hope, eventually I'll stop writing about things that make me sad, and start writing about things that haven't happened yet. I hope you'll feel bold from the tattoo ink on your skin.
I hope we can be friends.

Apathetic in a new way

I closed my eyes and plugged my ears before crossing the road
and never clutched my keys in my knuckles whenever a man slowed.
Spat my gum on the grass beside my garden's pitiful tree stumps
and gave up brushing my hair till it fell out in ugly clumps.
Played auntie once a month, hoping they'd forget my face
and played daughter at the dinner table, while shrinking in my space.
Wore the same knitted jumper until it stunk of smoke and sweat
and browsed fast fashion at 3am, resisting buying something I'd
regret.

Until sitting in your car, saying nothing, radio playing,
letting the world go on without me, I felt like staying.

Honestly, I'm frightened

You drop by unexpected,
finding me on my doorstep
in a tea-stained t-shirt that used to smell like you.
Your laundry powder is masked
by banana bread and cigarettes.

And I want to remember this.
Your fancy-pants phone voice when you first answer my hello.
My hands in your hair as you lay in my lap.
Your reckless driving that makes me feel alive.
My cold hands warm against your rings.
Smoking fags out your window.
Listening to one band in the car and another in your bedroom.
Introducing me to your friends, who already know all about me.
Making me dinner when I'm trying my best to eat.

But when I go back to bed,
part of me wants to bury these moments
far down where I can't reach them.
And wanting to go back to before
I knew I had you.
When every tell-tale sign you liked me,
I could deny and pretend I wasn't interested.
The playlist you made me,
when you thought I could die.
The tickets you almost booked,
that took me all summer to agree to.
The pity calls once or twice
when we were both bored and lonely.

Sometimes it feels like I took all that for granted.
Having you as a friend
but overthinking every conversation.
I guess I'm just scared of fucking this up
and losing everything.

Finally

It's come down to boredom and dissatisfaction,
witnessing your own life with zero reaction.

Adding sugar to your coffee when you crawl or leap out of bed,
taking long walks without the feeling of existential dread.

Feeling better but more like a stranger than yourself,
counting days where you feel something as a symbol of wealth.

And the days where you don't, well that's the tell-tale sign
that you were right, you'll never be more than just fine.

But at least you're existing,
in a life of either persisting or resisting.

Sorry isn't the right word, but

I think I took it too far
when I became obsessed with dancing
in your flames.
Monopolising your reckless calefaction,
I forgot that a burning house isn't
A bright beginning
but an ending to something
devastating.
Eating your embers up
like cereal,
spoon stirring your fragile heart
to rebuild my tragic self-worth.
Burnt out palettes
piling up,
a bonfire in the making
with you
the villainised victim on the stake.

www.ingramcontent.com/pod-product-compliance
Lightning Source LLC
LaVergne TN
LVHW052106160826
845678LV00015B/3393

* 9 7 9 8 8 3 8 9 6 7 9 0 9 *